The Road to
Dis MASK Me

(My Father's Mistress)

Tweedy Thomas

Dedication

This Book is dedicated to the millions wearing a mask from rape, molestation, mental and physical abuse. The hurt is deep, the pain is real but you don't have to fake it till you make it, you can survive. I pray this book will encourage you to face the truth take the mask off and live. You can get through it, get over it, and live life to the fullest.

I did, *(without the mask)!*

Thank you

Thank you God for prophecy being fulfilled. To my amazing husband Fred, who has supported me from day one. You have allowed me to tell my story as you sit proudly on the side, babe I love you. To my awesome children Marvin (Kea), Marchelle (Jason), C.J. (Demetra), you have always been there for mek, thanks, mama loves you. Thank you Dream Team, Monique Jeffery, Shayla Beck-Smith and Satoya Hemphill. You ladies are amazing. I made it. To the greatest church family on this side of glory God Is Ministries. Thanks for loving me.

Table of Contents

Introduction

Introduction

What do you do when it's a family member or close friend hurting you and they have convinced you that if you speak out, no one will believe you, if you tell anyone it will destroy you and your family.

God why would you allow this to happen to me? Where is He (God) in the mist of this storm that I have had to endure for way too long?

The only way to survive this nightmare is to wear a mask, so ten years ago I put on a mask.

What is a mask you may ask? Well a mask is something to conceal you from view or maybe something to keep unwanted views and opinions out.

I've worn a mask for so long that it has become a part of my face. It's just as important as my makeup. I put it on each time I go out to work, church, or social gatherings. It has become me.

But I'm tired of being the great pretender. Always acting like I have it all together and pretending nothing bothers me. And yet, I am dying on the inside.

This mask has to come off! I've questioned myself over and over again...What's behind the mask? Will I recognize who I really am? Will I even like me?

It would be so much easier to keep the mask on, but if I do that I'll miss out on all that God has for me.

To even begin the process of taking off the mask, I have to look deep into where I've been and how I ended up on this road.

What do you do when you know this secret will

destroy your life and your family?

What do you do when you feel God can't hear you and you are all alone, no one to talk too no one to trust or even believe in you?

A lot of questions that need answers.

I didn't say anything for a long time. I just continued to be the great pretender.

The hardest part will be facing who I was and how I became who I am.

When you hear my story you'll understand why.

This is not just my story, but an unspoken story of many that dare to or not to tell.

My cry is, "Lord, "Dis-MASK-me," help me to take this mask off.

MY MASK

Elements of the mask: LAYERS

The mask I created to shield myself is kind of like a make-up. Every layer and every element played a big part on how I put on the mask, how I wore it, and how I maintained it.

I'd wash my face, and as I washed my face I would try to wash away all the pain and hurt, just like it washed away my innocence.

I'd layer on my primer to prep and protect myself, and I may have thought I was protecting myself but in all honesty, I was building a wall. See, primer is like a shield so that you won't be exposed to things that may hurt you. Because you believe if someone or something cannot touch the surface directly it cannot affect you directly. But pain can come in indirect and direct ways no matter how much primer you layer on it, it always finds a way of touching you.

I'd layer my foundation to cover up. I would practice covering everything up, and as I grew older it got easier and easier. Hey what can I say, practice makes perfect! It had been happening for so long I taught myself how to hide my feelings. I had gotten so good at covering myself nobody could see the scars and the imperfections that were indebted in my heart.

To maintain the mask you must keep adding on things to make it fit you. So, when I started to grow I also started outgrowing the mask. The old layers I built started to fall apart once God began to manifest himself in my life. Now to keep myself and my mask from exposing a part of me I wanted to hide away, I had to keep adding on layers.

So, I'd layer on the concealer, when I put on my

concealer there would be a light and a dark. The light was my happiness and brightness while the dark was for, well the darkness. I would highlight the parts of my life I wanted everyone to see. Everyone would see the brilliant God gifted singer but I would contour the dark parts I wanted to keep locked up.

I'd layer on the blush to where you couldn't see how harsh the darkness was. It made the light and the dark separate, but blend so smooth. Blush is always warm, pinkish and sweet, it kept my darkness mellowed. Although the concealers gave me dimension to my mask, the blush blended out the rough edges and made everything come together. So, people only embraced my smooth light side, but over looked and could not see the darkness.

Then along the road, I added some personal touches to my mask. The glow, the lipstick, and the eye shadow. This was my personality and I could change it as many times as I wanted to. I named my mask 'TAM' because as Jenny was uncovered, Tam would always outshine her.

My Situation

I will never forget the day things started to change for me and my mother. I was walking outside and there stood old man Johnny yelling at my momma.

"You better tell Earl he still owes me for you." Mr. Johnny said, just as I opened the screen door.

Momma turned to me and said, "Get back in that house and don't come out until I tell you to."

I walked back in the house, but stayed by the door because, I wanted to know what was going on.

"Now, I don't know what you are talking about Johnny so you best tell me the whole story," momma said.

I heard Mr. Johnny laughing and say, "Why are you trying to play me for a fool? You have to know what I do for a living, everybody does. I am the local witch doctor and about ten years ago, Earl came to see me because he wanted you."

I could hear the trembling in my momma's voice when she said, "Get away from here with that nonsense, Johnny."

"I ain't leaving til I have had my say and finish telling the whole story." He replied

"Didn't you ever wonder why you married Earl? You didn't really like him and he wasn't the kind of man you dated so what was different about him? I will tell you what was different I placed a root on you just for him."

"I made you bond to him like glue. Earl brought me a pair of your dirty stockings and I did my mojo. You couldn't shake him even if you wanted to." (*things happen when you walk out of the will of God*)

"So again, I'm telling you to tell Earl, I want the rest of my money because he owes me for you."

A few seconds later I heard momma walking towards the door. I ran to the couch so that she wouldn't know I had heard the conversation. When she came into the house, I could see the pain and confusion on her face.

Her eyes, however told a different story. They revealed an acceptance I couldn't understand as a child.

Momma asked me, "If I was okay" and said for me to go outside all without looking in my direction.

I asked, "Momma, are you alright?"

"Sure, baby go on outside if you want" was her reply as she started walking down the hall.

I waited until I heard the bedroom door close.

Then I tiptoed up to the door and I heard my

momma crying out to God.

"Lord, I'm so sorry for not following your will. Lord, I'm sorry for not staying connected to you, but Lord, I need your help and I need you to get me and my baby out of this mess."

That was the day I realized my mother had been destroyed just as I had been for the past ten years.

While I had been my stepfather's mistress, he had been using my mother as well. One man had damaged us both.

What kind of man ensnares a woman with witchcraft and then takes the innocence of a little girl. A man with girls of his own, but he chooses me to make living a nightmare?

Mr. Earl and Dorothy

Tall 6' 2 stout, bald head, and dark complexion with big hunting eyes. Not very attractive but he sure had a way with words. The folk around town use to say ol' Earl could talk a woman out of her panties and make her think she still had them on. A retired disabled, military man so he said. He had been married multiple times and had several children, looking for his next prey. Low and behold he found it, my mom Sister Dorothy Jean Hunt. A sight for sore eyes standing 5'2, 130 pounds and all the right curves in all the right places, with that smooth caramel complexion. A church going God fearing woman, faithful member of White City Holiness Church. A struggling mom with two boys, Archie and Buddy and a young girl Jenny. Looking for love in all the wrong places. If truth be told she was a money woman, she didn't date a man unless he had some money and that Mr. Earl G. Hampton had.

Earl drove a really nice black deuce and a quarter car and drew an even nicer check from being disabled. Everything about this man looked good standing on the outside looking in but, oh on the inside he was a time bomb. Mom said the day they were to get married she woke up wanting to run away but, something wouldn't let her. It was like something had a hold on her and she couldn't shake it. So marry Earl she did, Mr. Earl and Mrs. Dorothy Hampton.

There's nothing worse than a person with a reprobated mind and Earl was a reprobate. He started off as the perfect husband and father, taking my brothers and I to school every day, making sure dinner was ready for my mom and the family. Earl was an excellence cook, he mastered the skill in the military as the mess hall cook. Checks were rolling in monthly and we had everything we could want for. Money in the bank, cars in the front yard, fine name brand clothes, you name it, we had it. But something just wasn't right, Mom acted like she was shame of Earl. That's when we realized Earl's health was going bad, in and out of the hospital he wouldn't eat right. He loved fried greasy food and this lead to him becoming a diabetic. So he began to go partially blind and his limbs began to deteriorate .

Mom would invite Earl to church but somehow he never made it. He'd say he was going and ask mom to get his clothes ready for Sunday service but when Sunday came he would back out. He was a backslider that knew the word and could quote the scripture by heart, book, verse and chapter. This is how I knew he had a reprobated mind for sure.

Something in him wanted to go to church but couldn't. *(Romans 1:28 "And even as they did not like to retain God in their knowledge, God gave them over to a reprobate mind, to do those things which are not convenient").*

*E*ventually, Mom just gave up on trying to get Mr. Earl to go to church with her. That was fine with me because I didn't want to have to hold his hand and lead him around anyway. Mr. Earl was really nice to me, he gave me almost everything and anything I wanted plus some. I didn't know it then but, later I would learn why.

My brothers received the same treatment, looks like Dorothy Jean has hit a gold mine. Finally the time has come for the boys to spread their wings. Archie the oldest gets married and moves to Big D; while the middle boy Buddy a few years later joins the Military.

The nest is almost empty but one, Me, my mom's pride and joy, the only girl. Now the real Earl Hampton shows up. I'm all alone no one to watch out for me and now the games began.

Jenny Jean

Born Jenny Jean Hunt, (my mom's maiden name), I guess my mother and biological father were never married. So I was raised by my mom and brothers until she married my stepfather, Mr. Earl G. Dottson.

I'm six years old, chocolate, big brown eyes with glasses, short in statue but on the thick side. We live in a one story white wooden house where you can step in the front room and see all the way to the back door. It's funny when I think about it the bathroom was on what we called the back porch and the living room and bed room were in the same room. My mom had a sofa on one side of the room and twin beds on the other side, with a big chair and lamp on the side.

I guess her and Earl actual slept in separate beds.

My brothers and I slept in the middle room, two beds, one on each side of the room. I didn't have a bed of my own, my oldest brother and I shared a bed when he was home. The third room was the kitchen and the big back porch were the bathroom and storage was. My brothers were much older than me so it felt like I was an only child when the boys left home. My closest friends were our neighbors who were up in age. There was Mama Clarise and her husband Boy, *(that's what I called him, I never knew Boy's real name)*, who lived directly across the street. And Mama and Papa Larkins right next door with the pretty white picket fence. They told me the day my mom got saved in a prayer meeting at the house, Mama Larkins heard the noise, "came to see what was going on and was filled with the holy spirit the moment she walked in the door".

Mama Clarise and Mama Larkin were my babysitters until my mom married Earl.

My mom worked a lot, a whole lot and left me at home with my step dad. Her life consisted of work, church and more work and church but, Earl never went to church or work. As long as that check came in every month mom was fine. My mom was so busy working, churching and spending money, that she didn't notice me much. I don't know and will never know what it's like to be a little girl, play like a little girl, think or act like a little girl. There has always been an anointing on my life I would pray for sick people and they would be healed but all this was short lived after Earl came along. I never was given the chance to be a little girl any more after my brothers left home. As far back as I can remember starting at the tender age of six, when my brothers left home, my stepfather Earl became a nightmare.

I will never forget that day...

"Go behind the chair and pull down your panties and let me feel, it won't hurt." Earl whispered, he gave me that certain look and I knew something was wrong, it did not feel right. But, what do I know I'm just a kid.

I went behind the chair in the living room and pulled down my panties. I didn't know what I was doing or what was coming next but, I knew not to disobey. I was scared of whippings and my mama didn't play about being disobedient. Nobody was home we were alone, Earl and I in the house. So, even if I did attempt to disobey or scream nobody would have heard me anyway. It would have been his word against mine.

I pulled my panties down and he processed to take his finger and touch my vagina, invading the space between my legs.

He didn't care that it actually hurt or that it was uncomfortable he just wanted to get his freak on. Was he supposed to be doing this, I thought? I'm scared stiff, I can't move we are looking eye to eye well, not really because, his eyes are closed. 'Mama Help, come get me' I'm screaming in my head. I don't know how long this went on maybe a few minutes but it felt like hours to me. That is how it all started for me. This is where the mask came on. He would fondle me at every opportunity he could and there were many. Where was my mom while all this was going on? Oh yeah at church, my mom would sometimes be at work or other times as close as her bedroom resting or sleep, trusting the man she married.

Why didn't I scream you may ask; I couldn't. Fear has a way of taking even your small voice of crying out away.

I was too scared, scared of getting a whipping, scared of him , and really scared of my own mom. More than anything scared that no one would believe me and think I was a bad child. I cannot, will not mess up my mother's reputation. People just love her, hum everybody loves Sister Dorothy Hunt Hampton.

See my step father, Earl, had already told me that if I told my mom or anybody else what we were doing three things would happen. Number one, they would not believe me, number two mom would be so mad at me and number three he would kill us all. So you see I couldn't afford to tell anybody, scared and shamed I kept our little nasty secret.

As a young child in my day, you believed what grown folk told you. Especially when that someone is a person you are told to respect and obey. In my mind he was right, this was my fault. I was doing something to attract his attention in this way. I need to figure out whatever it is I'm doing and stop it right now. Lord I wish my brothers was here. I need someone to stop this merry go round I want to get off.

By the time I was eight years old the abuse has gotten worst. It has gone from taking my panties off behind the chair and putting his finger in me, to coming into my bedroom when my mom went to sleep.

By this time we've moved to a bigger house where I was easier access for Earl because, I have my own room now. My mom is so impressed with our big, roomy ranch style house. It sat on a corner lot with several bedrooms and a couple of bathrooms. My room is in the back of the house, how convenient for old Earl. There were nights he would actually get in bed with me, which made me sick to my stomach. I was so scared mom was going to wake up looking for him but, she never did. (Shame on her!)

I can't count the nights I've been awaken by Earl with my breast in his hands or his hand between my legs.   What's a child to do?

Three years have passed I am nine years old, I have started my cycle and my breast is fully developed into a 34b, with that round tight butt. WOW, a nine year old with the body of a 13 year old. I'm stacked yes Lord, the apple didn't fall far from the tree.

And I thought my lesser developed body caught his attention with all these assets added, Earl was having a field day! Breast bigger, butt bigger, legs thick, can't my mom see something is wrong? (*Wake up mother something wrong is going on right under your nose.*)

NO! She's too busy working on her job, to busy working in the church, she can't see this blind, reprobated mind, person. (*Roman 1:28*) I feel invisible to her, how can you over look someone you see every day and can't recognize the changes that are taking place right before your eyes. *(Is it you can't see or you don't want to see.)*

To make matters even worse I have to call this man, my mother's husband, 'Daddy'! *(I know what I want to call him' Daddy Demon.')*

One night, it wasn't just a regular night, this night it wasn't just a hand on my breast or a feel between my legs, it was my virginity being taken by force, while my mother slept peacefully in another room. It hurt so bad, tears rolling down my face, I tried to holler 'stop' but, he covered my mouth with his hand to keep me from screaming out.

This night Earl has stolen something from me. My virginity had been taken, I didn't lose it, it was taken without my permission or consent. Violated stripped of my innocence, something I can never get back, I am scared forever. I'm thinking to myself, nobody will ever want me now! And all he can say is, "you better wash them sheets before your mama find them."

Blood stained sheets, tear stained eyes.

Innocence gone no more mama's little girl.

Think about this, my sleeping partner is "daddy" and I've become his mistress.

Can you imagine losing your virginity to a man that is supposed to be your father? The very person you should be able to trust, the person that's supposed to protect you! I am so confused.

(If you can't trust your parent who can you trust? No One! Absolutely No One!)
MASK ON.

This was my life for several years. A school girl by day and my father's mistress by night!
(I saw that you just had a flash back. It's ok that is the only way we are going to work through where we've been, we have to face it. It's ugly but we are not hiding any more)
The Mask must come off!

I felt so ashamed, but who could I really talk to. No one would ever believe me. I had a few church friends but, I would not dare tell them. Momma always said, "WHAT GOES ON IN OUR HOUSE STAYS IN OUR HOUSE!" So it is, what it is.. Scared lonely, abused…

The nights he left me alone I felt relieved, I cried silent tears wondering "What I could do differently?"

Maybe I could change the way I dressed or the way I talked. What was I doing to draw his attention?" Nothing was going to change this dog but death. *OK,* so how could I kill him without hurting my mom?

(have you ever thought about killing something before it killed you?)

Going to church every Sunday morning and every Wednesday night, not one adult could see the pain I was in or the shame that I was made to carry because no one wanted to see. People were too busy to notice the small tears I shed for no reason or the withdrawal I had from other children my age. All the church folk who claimed to hear from God, but they never heard him for me. Which made me wonder was there really a God, and was he really concerned about me. But, I read in the Word of God that He would never leave me nor forsake me, (Deuteronomy 31:6) so why do I fell so alone? One day, my mother decide to go out and leave me again with my stepfather but this time I have had enough. Out of nowhere I finally got the courage to beg my mom not to leave me at home alone with Earl. Please mama take me with you please, don't leave me here please, please I cried! When she asked why not, I broke down scared, crying, and shaking. Something in me blurtod out everything that has been going on for the past 3 long years.

And just like Earl said she didn't believe me. At first, she asked me why I would make up such nonsense on a man that was being a father to me, taking such good care of us. Very stern and cold mama looked in my eyes and said 'why you doing this to us'? .

Then my mom got mad at my silence and she reached for that big leather belt and whipped me real good. She said she whipped me because if it was true I should have told her sooner, but what difference would it have made.

All I could do was stand there and cry as realization came, this is going to be my life forever. If my own mom doesn't believe me, who would?

I don't know if my mom ever confronted him *(I doubt it) be*cause she continued to leave me with him. So why did I break my silence, it was all for nothing because she didn't leave him and the sexual abuse continued.

I need a hiding place, God can you hear me?

Freedom Shorted Lived

Two (2) years later mom leaves Earl for another man. She started dating this construction worker, who rented a room from us while working in our little county town.

He was a tall dark and stocky guy by the name of Mr. Slim Jim, that's what everyone called him. Slim Jim seemed to be a quiet guy but all the time he was hitting on my mom behind Earl back. This dude must have been a smooth talker to convince my mom to leave her gold mine Earl. But, before I knew it, we were moving from the county going to the big city. *(So long bye bye old Earl with your nasty self)*. That's how we got to 'Big D' Dallas. A fresh start, is all I wanted. Mama must have wanted it as bad as I did because we were living in an apartment and she seems happy. I didn't too much like Slim Jim

either. *(something just didn't set right with me)*
But I was just so happy that I was finally free I
thought.

Then one night Slim approached me asking if he
could touch my breast. He said Earl had told him
all about me and him and he wanted in on the
action. I told him try it if you want to, I'm going
to call the police this time. I done got tired
(in my Ma-Dear voice), I am ready to fight back.
I don't' know how but I am not going through
this with another one of my mama's men.

We had one car and mom would take Mr. Slim
Jim to work and pick him up every day. I will
never forget, one day mom went to pick Slim
Jim up from work and he wasn't there. She asked
around the construction site and one of the guys
told her Slim had left with another woman.
What mama didn't know was Mr. Slim Jim was

running too. Running from a bad relationship of witch craft and voodoo but, his old lady had found him and came to take back her man. And that she did. *(I guess it didn't help that I had told Slim Jim I was going to call the po-po on him.)*

It wasn't long before we fell on hard times. My freedom was short lived, hurt, broken, angry, mom went back to what was familiar to her. Old boy done left mom, and she went back to our hometown and did the unthinkable, brought Earl back to live with us in the city.

We moved from the Southern Apartments to a really nice house on Fordham Rd. Mom must feel safe again and Earl is grinning from ear to ear. I must have screamed on the inside so loud that I thought I heard it echo from the walls of the house. Because you already know what's up (Ya, *you guessed it!)*

I'm the mistress again, just like old times.

My stepdad becomes a regular visitor to my bed.

And my mom couldn't see it or wouldn't see it.

 I hate HIM, I hate her, I hate them. Who do I hate the most, *my mom for allowing all of this to be done to me or Earl for doing it to me?*

 I had to learn to forgive, (we'll talk about that later).

From the moment my mom picked Earl up and brought him to Dallas with us, I knew with all my heart and everything in me that Jenny was dead. Jenny the girl that was her daddy's mistress and it seemed as though that was the way it was going to always be. MASK on!

(For every testimony there is a test even when you don't know the test will become a testimony.)

TAM

The day Jenny gave up after feeling like she was fighting a losing battle, Tam evolved out of Jenny's death. The only way Jenny could survive was to die and take on a another identity, a mask *we will call* **'TAM'.** Now Tam did not play games and she didn't take no mess at least that's what I thought. Tam was Jenny's mental mask to hide the shame, guilt, hurt, and anger. Tam became my hiding place. *(Have you ever allowed yourself to become someone else just to make it through.)*

Jenny died at the precious age of twelve and Tam is now in the driving seat. Tam didn't play that. Tam thought if she had to endure this man then she was going to benefit from it. "Why not use him like he was using our body."

Tam became the dominate person in my mind.

This girl could sing her butt off and play that tambourine. She was strong, courageous, had a I care, I don't care attitude, and didn't take nothing from no body. She had an answer for everything and didn't mind telling it like it is. Very out spoken and mama would say 'you so sarcastic'. The sarcasm was a cover for the unspoken feelings we had inside.

Tam never thought what Earl was doing was right. But, she had to find a way to expose him without bringing shame to the family mostly mom. Mom's reputation in the church was important, she was the usher board president, pastor's aide president, and the mothers board president.

We attended church as a family faithfully, *(Earl not included)* and I just knew that everything would come out if I kept going at least I did for a while. Until I realized folk in the church were too busy in their own affairs to see a little messed up girl like me. Yes everyone praised me for the voice I had and the ability to play that tambourine but who noticed the pain. *(No One)*

Yes, Yes! Tam was the church girl everybody liked. A faithful member of Born Again Tabernacle Church, singer, choir director, youth director and could play the skin off that tambourine. But one thing was wrong Tam hung around too many boys. Every time you looked up she was in some little boy's face. And because Tam only hung out with the boys the church folk would talk about her and often say that, "She just so fast honey," as they call it, Sister Dorothy better watch her. "Oh that Tam is a hott mess," the older sisters in the church would say. They had no clue.

They had no idea that the boys in our life were our protection. These good, God fearing, holy roller, church folks had no idea that as long as I was with the fellas, my stepfather didn't have the opportunity to try and have sex with me. The guys were welcomed at our home any time, come early stay late if you wanted too. Mama went to work at 3pm and didn't get off till 11pm. We needed the company. There were a few girls in our life we just had to be very protective of them We knew we couldn't have any girls as friends because we were too scared that what Earl was doing to us he would try to do to them. So we kept the girls away.

Tam is so smart. Once she figured out that as long as people were around us, the less time we had together with Earl and he couldn't make us sleep with him.
She made sure that the guys just hung around the house till mom got home from work and

then we were safe.

Tam with the Voice, Tam with the Tambourine.
Tam sing and play girl sing and play. Play the
shame away.

It was strange that none of the church folk
seemed to inquire about the real reason as to
why I'm always with these boys. I would sit in
church and pray that a prophet would prophecy
to me and tell the whole church our little
family's dirty secret. But that never happened,
they wanted to always talk about the beautiful
voice but they never could see the pain.

GOTTA TELL YOU THIS

Once I thought my mom had finally accepted the
truth and discovered I really was telling the truth
all these years about her dear old hubby Earl.
One nice sunny evening, I was in the door way

of mama's room, Earl had called me. Mama was standing behind me in the hall leading to her bedroom out of sight. She was in the shadows where Earl couldn't see her and I thought for sure she overheard a conversation he and I had *(he was talking I was listening)*.

He's in their room sitting in the chair gazing out the window when he hears me come into the room. He says to me "ha you can walk around with no clothes on now that I'm sick and partially blind, I don't mind." Now I know she heard that, I looked back over my shoulder and she looks down at the floor. *(sometimes we think if we ignore something it will go away, well guess what it does not)* I spoke up and said that's all right, I'll keep my clothes on. You see Earl had been diagnose with sugar diabetes and was losing his sight, a few toes had been amputated but his mind was still reprobate. You would think he would be trying to get his life right but Oh no, not Earl! I was startled when I saw mom step up behind me and asked Earl "what did you say?" He laughed and played it off but I know she heard him.

Tam was giving me life again, making this nasty little secret work for us. We had everything and anything a girl could want for, (*it's called hush money*)

Valentine Letter

Eventually, I get myself a boyfriend. Sam Gibbs star student, handsome guy standing 5'10. He was slim built, with those dreamy eyes, smooth chocolate skin and a voice that makes you listen. O' and by the way he's a church boy, a little preacher actually. His older sister goes to the church where mom and I attend. So I get to see him not only at school but, when he comes to visit his sister at the church. I'm a really good singer, so sometimes he invites me to come with him when he goes out to speak. That's really cool, I get to sing before my boyfriend preach. Things are going really good for a while I thought. I had learn how to avoid Earl or bride him out of his money. *(If you know what I mean If you can't beat them you join them).*

You do something for so long until it doesn't matter anymore if it's right or wrong, you just do it.

I was real active, singing and directing the choir at church and a cheerleader at school. I would do just about anything to keep me away from the house. Life was looking up I had a boyfriend, and I was doing really good in school and church. I had learn to mask the pain, hurt and anger in public so no one knew the wiser.

Then disaster strikes, the one thing no girl wants to admit, I got dumped. My boyfriend broke up with me on Valentine's Day of all days. I'm devastated, I cannot believe this, please God not today, any other day but today. Valentine's Day when love is suppose to be in the air, everyone is giving and receiving gifts and I received a pretty big pink fluffy teddy bear with a dear john or should I say a dear Jenny letter.

I'm sitting on the side of my bed reading this, *Dear Tam, let me start by saying Happy Valentine's Day, I have truly enjoyed being with you, getting to know you and spending time with you. The pass days, weeks, months have been a blast and I want you to know this is so hard for me. Because of my love for God and you, I have to say good bye. I don't know how to tell you this without making you angry or upset but I can't see you anymore. I feel I am being pressured to do something I am not ready to do right now. So before I mess up with you and God, I will just say "good bye."* As tears stream down my face I don't know what to feel or think. Holding this letter in one hand and the phone in the other I call Sam I need answers. What is he talking about being pressured to do something he's not ready to do?

When Sam answers the phone we hold the

phone in silence for a minute until I can get myself together. I tell him I want answers why are you doing this? That's when I learn my dad was trying to get Sam to have sex with me. And he respected me too much for that but, the pressure of my father was getting to him so it was better to leave me alone. "What's wrong with that dude anyway," he asked, What father encourages a boy to try and sleep with their daughter. I am blown lose. What the h**! Sam takes a deep breath and said 'I really feel sorry for you."

Oh you heathen! So to cover up what you been doing to me you try to drag somebody else into this. You low down dirty dog you! I cried and cried but Tam told me don't worry she would fix it.

 I don't know if mama heard me crying or screaming into the phone but she rushed into my room with this confused look on her face. While closing the door behind her she looked at the huge balloon and teddy bear my daddy*(hmm)* had brought me and she asked "girl what's wrong with you?" I couldn't say a word I just handed her the letter.

This man has been riding me like a horse with no saddle since I was only six years old, will this ever end? Is there a God if so where is He? Lord I need you now!

Maybe I should try talking to an older guy, somebody who can stand up to Earl. That's it, that's exactly what I'll do, get involved with someone older. Lafayette Chanschez, 21 years old, nice car, not so nice looking and ask no questions. He knows I'm too young to go out, so we always end up at his house, in his bed.

Mama use to say the best way to get over one man is to get another one.

(sometimes a girls gotta do what a girl gotta do)

Lord you have to help me I'm out of control. So many questions and yet so much devastating pain. Would God really let something like this continue to happen to a young girl? I'm innocent! What did I do to deserve this?

Where do you go when you feel like there's no one to turn too? I felt as though no one cared enough to seek God concerning me. Where are the prophets, can't anyone see behind the mask? Can anyone see what my soul and heart really looks like?

Almost Got Caught

The day my mom almost caught us (Earl and I) in her bed having sex, I was 15 years old.

She left me at home with Earl again, while she went on vacation with another man John Porter. A man better than what she had, but still another man. There's one thing I can give my mom credit for, she always told me where she was going and who she was with.

Earl is no fool. He knows my mom really don't love him but they are together, her for the money and security and him for the sex (me). So, he really don't care how often or long she stays gone, it just gives him more time with me.

A lot of things have changed over the course of nine years, I know my role and have accepted it. I know I will be Earl's mistress until one of us died. I don't dread sex with Earl as bad anymore,

I kinda like what I'm feeling but, he's still nasty. He keep telling me I can't get pregnant because he can't have any more babies so what is there to worry about?

It was a nice quite Saturday evening the front door is open but, the screen door is locked.

I hadn't had a chance to get out of the house, mom was gone on her little rendezvous, and I'm in my room chilling. I can hear old Earl getting restless. He calls me into their bedroom and start asking me a lot of questions about nothing. That's his way of getting around to asking can I have some. So Tam says "if I give you some, what you gonna give me?" Earls thinks for a few minutes and replies "I'll buy you that purse you been wanting". DEAL! So I laid across his bed *(this not gonna take long)* Earl was on top of me and I was telling him to hurry up I had something else to do. See by this time I could get anything I wanted from daddy Earl, clothes, shoes, money anything, everything. (*It was called hush don't tell on me money*).

Tam figured that if I didn't tell what we were doing then he would give me whatever I ask for. And I made it my business to ask for a lot. Tam's idea was never give without getting. Any time we give we get.

(*I know this memory is tough but until we face who we have become we will never be who we should be.*)

We heard a noise at the front door, Oh shoots, Oh my God, Lord it's my mama trying to get into the house. But the front screen door is locked and there were some baby kittens on the porch. "Wow," my mom was scared of kittens so, she began to scream for help, 'Earl come get these cats'! This is almost funny, right in the middle of him about to explode, he hears my mother screaming. You talk about scared to death! Earl almost died on top of me.

Earl jumped up and ran to the bathroom, sweating like a pig, shaking like a leaf on a tree and booboo running everywhere. (*It may not have scared him to death but it scared the booboo out of him.lol*)

He told me to go to my room and pretend like I was asleep and couldn't hear my mom knocking and screaming. I let my mother call my name a few times before daddy Earl eventually gave me the cue to get up and go to the door to let her in. I was yawning and stretching like I had been asleep.

By now, I'd been trained well. I almost enjoy this game.

God was truly with us that day. He planted those kittens on the porch just so mom would not catch her man and his mistress, her fifteen year old daughter in her bed. *I don't know how she would have handled that but I'm sure someone would have been dead that day.*

I had reached a point in my mind when I realized my mom was never going to believe me and Earl was never going to stop. So we had no other choice but to take matters into our own hands.

Jenny felt like she had slowly lost the battle. Never the less Tam had put her mind and energy into coming up with a way to kill Earl by the time they finished high school. *(a double minded man is unstable in all his ways)* Tam kept singing , "Earl, you have 2 years before you are dead and we are FREE!" We chanted this every day, "Two years till I'm free -no more chains holding me"

Dis- MASK

Before I could get free an awesome opportunity presented itself, I was asked to travel with a gospel choir. I was going to Hot Lanata with the Mitchell Street Pentecostal Church choir, I was only sixteen. I begged mama to let me go and she did. On the road, all alone, no real family to watch over me. But, who cares, I knew it was cowardly, but I was running and we had to take that chance. It was the only way we could get free. So Tam sang at every engagement the church had and stayed on the road for as long as she could.

It seemed ages before we got back home but, it was only for a couple of weeks and we was able to see mama again.

Finally we could breathe a little. The Mask is

starting to come off .

Jenny was long gone by now and only Tam remained and she was ecstatic.

Earl had taught her a lesson about men and Tam was using everything she was taught to her advantage. It wasn't long before she was able to get men to do whatever she wanted them to do for a little nookie.

And best believe Tam flaunted, flirted, and shimmied. Sex had become the currency she used by choice subconsciously because that was all she knew. She was what they called the church whore *(yes, they still exist today)*. It's not that they are true whores. Some of them are just like me, we have baggage and don't know any other way. We don't need a lot of friends, we don't trust anybody and we are angry.

But, if you really think about it, sex was all I knew to barter with.

Tam had been using it on Earl for five plus years. This new way of life became the norm for her and she was enjoying it until, she got us pregnant. It's time for a change. This Mask must come off. We have been really looking for love and acceptance all in the wrong places.

That John Porter guy that mom went on vacation with turned out to be a good one for mama. He loved her unconditional and was willing to help her with no strings attached. It wasn't long after that my mom finally left Earl for good. Sent him packing back to the country where he belonged. They tell me old Earl died cursing folks out, *(I didn't get to kill him after all looks like God did it for me.)*

Mr. Porter said I could call him Papa John and that was fine with me. Finally a real man was in our life. Someone I could respect and look up too, someone to show me what a real daddy is suppose to be about. Papa John made life so much easier for me. I didn't have to sleep with one eye open and one eye closed. *(Could this be God working for me now?)* Now we went to church as a real family me, Mom and Papa John.

That was when Jenny tried to reassert herself back to life and started wanting a real relationship with God. I'm singing but, am I listening to the words coming out of my mouth? "Where can I turn, Who can I talk to, Who do I lean on, I go to the rock, that rock is Jesus." Now don't get we wrong, Tam had a relationship with God but, not a deep connection with God. Because she was still angry and bitter, she couldn't see the why in all we had went through. To Tam all men were good for was to have sex with and pay bills, period.

They all act and talk like they were true men of God, but they would play off on their wives for a little something, something. Shake your hand and put money in your hand at the same time.*(slick aw)*

And to top it off, most of Tam's men were church men. Deacons, Preachers, and some Pastors. And they paid well. Tam had the best clothes, shoes, cars, and always had some money in her hand bag. *One old slick preacher even told her, two clean sheep can't dirty each other. (what the H**)*

We could sing rings around anybody and was well known for our anointed voice. And please don't trip because, God can anoint you for His purpose and you still be in your mess. *(gifts can come without repentance Romans 11:29)*

But, God has his hand on us and our time to

surrender was approaching fast. It wasn't until God busted us and my son was born that things started to look different to Tam. We both knew we wanted our son to embrace being a man, a God fearing man, a King, a man of honor. The love that instantly engulfed me was awe inspiring. *(I'm saying we because at this space in life I am living a double life Tam & Jenny).*

Some changes have to be made. The spirit of the Lord is tugging at our heart.
Tam knew then that she had to cut lose this life style but, she didn't know how. There is only one way but, it's a process. A long dark process. A process of facing who we had become, what caused us to do the things we did, and facing the inner me. Anger with ourselves, old Earl, my Mom, the church, even God.
As we had begun the process of developing a

relationship with God, we realize that our actions now affect someone else. We cannot , we will not carry or allow all this hatred to spread. We are finally getting on the right track. We have to look at the woman in the mirror and ask her to allow God to change her ways.

(Jeremiah 17:14 heal me Lord and I shall be healed; save me and I shall be saved)

God had to reposition us.

The next step was forgiveness. I went to the father asking for forgiveness, but yet I still harbored unforgiveness. *(Mark 11:25 "If you have anything against anyone forgive him, that your Father in heaven may also forgive your trespasses.")*

So I had to forgive my mom for not putting an end to all the pain that was caused by her husband. Then I had to forgive Earl even though he was dead and couldn't ask for forgiveness.

The most important part of forgiving was really facing the things in which I had endured and participated in for 10 years. Forgiving myself was truly the hardest. Layer by layer taking off the layers of blush, primer and contour so you couldn't see how harsh the darkness was. Allowing the rough edges to show in order to be healed. Removing the concealers that gave me dimension to my mask and admitting my part in the wrong person I had become. I took off my personal touches, lipstick, eye shadow all the excuses I'd use to play and stay where I was.

Dis - MASK!

Dis MASKing required me to;

1. Face the man in the mirror (*look at yourself no really look, it's ok you are who you are*)

2. Accept and admit your part in the situation (*Admit how you feel and how it make you feel*)

3. Repent (*Confess, Lord I'm sorry please*

forgive me, I need you Lord.)

4. Forgive those that hurt you (*now this will be hard because they may not ask, deserve or even want to be forgiven, forgive any way, it's for you not for them.)*

5. Forgive yourSELF/ Let yourself off the hook (*this is the hardest, but you owe it to yourself to forgive yourself.)* Free Yourself!

Do as Paul did in Philippians 3:13 forgetting those things which are behind...

6. Talk about it out loud *(to someone you can trust; when you hear it out of your mouth it stops playing in your head.)*

Then Forget it..lose the memory of it

7. Don't look back and don't let anyone take you back. (*You can't always fix the past but you can out live it.)*

It's done you can't take it back so, reach forth unto those things which are before you and press forward. Now see yourself as God sees you say it out loud: (*I am who God says I am; I am the righteousness of God, I am more than a conqueror, I am the head and not the tail above only and not beneath.*) *It's over now LIVE!* There will be times when you have to repeat the steps and remind yourself you have overcome. It's alright, repeat as many times as needed just don't go back. I've learned when I can't go forward I just stand still.

Restoration

Once I became fully dedicated to God, I then had to become fully committed to the process. The process began not only with forgiveness but also with recognizing the anointing being placed upon me that I could not have imagined.

God had anointed me to sing, to play the tambourine, preach the gospel, and a beautiful smile. Oh, my tambourine, my sanity keeper. I'll never forget the times this instrument keep me in my right mind, it became my safe haven. I would play until the pain, and frustration went away. When I played I was no longer a victim of abuse, there was no shame, I was free, I was alive.

Now this preaching thing, I personally never wanted to preach the gospel because I knew the things I had done, the life I had lived and what I

was still doing, yet God had to redirect my path.
I truly loved God even though I had a ugly past.
I needed God to redirected my life. I never
wanted to infect other people with the poison of
anger and the hatred I felt for the male species. I
came to realize it wasn't men I hated so much as
it was intimacy. Intimacy had no meaning to me,
I only knew how to have sex. *(God had some
work to do.)*

*I had given up on relationships and was just
trying to stay faithful to God, my children and
myself.*

As time went on I had three beautiful children
and a few unsuccessful marriages. God allowed
me to meet an amazing man that I could open up
to and tell anything. I told him my good, not so
good, bad and the real bad. *(this got to be God)*
I'm ministered at this little church on the south
side of town; after service this dude walks up

and introduces himself and gives me this note with his phone number. *(The note reads' God told me whatever you need do it.')* I thought this man is tripping. I'm a big, (plus size) girl and have three babies, but okay dude.

I was in my early thirties and he was barely in his mid twenties, what could he offer me other than a little assistance with some bills.

(wasn't I in for a surprise)

It didn't dawn on me that God was going to use this man to restore my love, trust and intimacy with a man.

This man courted me the way a real man should. He brought me flowers for no reason, made me laugh, and he had me enjoying life for the first time in my life. He prayed with me, he prayed for me, he even started going to engagements with me.

I call myself seeing someone else and this dude

tells me "don't choose between him and the other dude because he knew what God had told him." (*What kinda guy is this?*)

The one thing he made me promise is, to never let my children wake up and find him in our home. *(He kept his promise.)*

Sitting around the kitchen table at my pastor's house, in blue jeans and t-shirts we said, "I DO."

God is so amazing , God used this man to allow me to be young again. I didn't want for anything, if I spoke it or even thought it he provided it. He restored my faith in man and gave my children and I a new life.

God loved me so much that He manifested his love for me in the form of my husband.

God restored to me everything the enemy had stolen and some.

And it all started to happen when I found my safety net in God, forgetting those things that were behind me and moving forward.

You see this game will go on forever until you sell out to God and allow Him to heal the hurt. Only then can He fulfill that deepest desire. The icing on the cake was that God included my kids in His plan of restoration for me. You see, a man took me from God and a man brought me back to God.

I want to encourage you to take the mask off and face your past, present and future. Come out of the closet and allow God to deliver and restore you. No, it won't be easy and you will have a few setbacks. Remember a setback is a set up to get us in the place God wants us to be.

God will surely make it worth your while.
Eye hath not seen, nor ear hear, neither have
entered into the heart of man, the things which
God hath prepared for them that love him.
1Corinthians 2:9 (KJV)

*(The Last thing I want you to do is look real
close you will see you are not the only one
wearing a mask.)*
God Bless you, beloved

PS
Oh by the way God restored my love and
relationship with my mom and we became the
best of friends. *(God never half do anything)*

Tweedy Thomas

After shattering strongholds of rape and molestation Tweedy Thomas, founded God Is Ministries in Desoto Tx. where she currently serves as the senior pastor. She also serves her community through the emergency food pantry, Healing Hand Food. Tweedy is a gospel singer, motivational speaker and overseer of Kingdom Connection Fellowship of Churches. She is known as the tambourine lady, the Internet Tambourine Sensation "Tweedy Time"

email:godisministry60@gmail.com

Made in the USA
Monee, IL
09 May 2021